DONKEY
DHARMA

THOUGHTS BY AND FOR
ENLIGHTENED PROGRESSIVES

Contents

Dedication
How This Book Came to Be
The First Donkey Dharma
Unions
Class Warfare
Hating President Obama
19th Century Social Policies
After the 2010 Midterms
We Got Him
Another Battle in Class Warfare
American Bigotry Travels to Norway
The Poor
Economic Mobility, but in What Direction?
Social Justice
Not Right, but Rather Cruel, Speech
Diversity
Elizabeth Warren
Right Speech and the Second Amendment
We're All Sikhs
The Politics of Jesus
Laughable … at First
Job-Creating Fund Raiser
Lilly Ledbetter
Still More Class Warfare
The Second Amendment
Profanity

Etch-a-Sketching the Truth
You Don't Have to be a Buddhist
Not a Traditional America Anymore?

Dedication

*May all sentient beings be
peaceful;*

May all sentient beings be happy;

May all sentient beings be safe.

*May all sentient beings awaken to
the light of their true nature.*

May all sentient beings be free.

(Tibetan Buddhist prayer)

How This Book Came to Be

Donkey Dharma began as part of a spiritual journey, and became part of the realization that the journey *is* the destination.

I was raised in the Byzantine Catholic Church. Its rich, deep, sonorous liturgy evoked awe, joy, and wonder. But, like everyone, as I grew I began to ask questions – typical questions like "What happened to all the people who ate meat on Fridays before the rules were changed?" Neither the Byzantine nor Roman churches had any answers, at least for me. They were the Mitt Romneys of their day, saying only "Trust us; we know what we're doing." That's a naggingly unsatisfying answer. And so my journey began. Ultimately, it took me to Buddhism.

Buddhism has been called "a religion without a God". To me, that's an asset. Christianity, Islam, and Judaism seem, at least, to emphasize worship over seeking wisdom; dogma and theology over practice; and the ability to affect positive change residing, not within oneself, but in some great unknown. Buddhism, on the other hand, has little if any dogma; takes a lyrically simple approach to such questions; emphasizes personal responsibility; and offers a set of guidelines that can be applied to every area of life. That spiritual roadmap is called the **Noble Eightfold Path**.

Phrased more colloquially, we could call it **Eight Steps to Enlightened Behavior**. The steps are:

- **Right Understanding** (looking at life and the world as they are, not as we would have them be)

- **Right Intention or Thought** (a commitment to good will and non-violence)

- **Right Speech** (defined in the Pali Canon, one of the sacred books of Budsdhism, as abstaining from lying, from divisive speech, from abusive speech, and from idle chatter or gossip)

- **Right Action** (refraining from actions that might bring harm to oneself or to others)

- **Right Livelihood** (refraining from trades or occupations that, directly or indirectly, harm other living beings)

- **Right Effort** (persisting in pursuing the first five steps on the Path)

- **Right Mindfulness** (being mindful and deliberate, making sure not to act or speak due to inattention or forgetfulness)

- **Right Concentration** (committed and mindful meditation)

Again speaking colloquially, we can translate **right** as *desirable* or *ideal*. That is, these eight steps are facets of behavior that, practiced in a committed way, cam lessen suffering and help to eradicate greed, hatred, and delusion.

At about the same time that I began to explore Buddhism, I was becoming a political junkie … ☺ The Presidential election of 2000, the completely false underpinnings of the Iraq war; Governor Howard Dean's Presidential campaign in 2004; the election of the first female Speaker of the House in 2006; the election of the first African-American President in 2008; the tsunami that was the Tea Party's takeover of the House of Representatives in 2010; and the bat-merde crazy policies and actions of the "new" AKA far far far right Republican Party, all pushed me toward anger, and activism. My efforts to follow the Path helped me deal with the anger. The Path, and in particular Right Speech and Right Action, helped give my activism focus.

Thus was born Donkey Dharma. It began as a blog and then morphed into a sequence of occasional hardcopy newsletters. The essays were eventually gathered into this book.

The collection is organized in chronological order, with the first essay dating from 2006, and the last from November 2012. The Table of Contents, however, lists them not by date but by topic.

It's my hope that reading this book will help you apply Right Speech and Right Action to improving our country and our world. You don't have to be a Buddhist to speak up for truth and fairness …

The First Donkey Dharma

North Braddock, a small town in southwestern Pennsylvania, was home to one of Andrew Carnegie's first steel mills. Just down the road in Braddock, one can still find his first Free Library. Growing up in North Braddock meant growing up with Pittsburgh the steel capital of the world. Sadly, much of what made it that has been lost, to the region and to the United States as a whole. What happened? Not-really-all-that-compassionate conservatives substituted parenthetical culture wars and economic shortsightedness for bread-and-butter issues and, ominously, for real moral values. Another way of putting it: these folks indulged in, large segments of the public bought, and from 2001 to 2006 Democrats failed effectively to counter, what Buddhists know as adharma.

Adharma can be defined as words or deeds that violate one's personal responsibility to the world and its inhabitants, from knowingly disobeying laws to littering. Adharma is the opposite, the inverse, of dharma. Dharma consists, essentially, of allowing one's actions to be driven by truth. Buddhists believe that actions based in adharma, in a false sense of the primacy of self, in an us-versus-them mentality, may succeed for a time, but will eventually bring about really bad stuff. Actions based in dharma, on the other hand, may take a bit longer to bear fruit, but will bear fruit that is solid. That's what this book deals in – the adharmic actions of neocon ideologues, and the actions based in dharma that progressives take or suggest. They're the bad guys; we're the good guys.

Uhm ... actually, the Buddha would frown on such distinctions, and consider them a moralistic source of personal pride. He would instead tell us that good and evil are interdependent. He'd note further that some of us don't feel we're good unless we're attacking perceived evil outside ourselves. Donkey Dharma will try to avoid such mistakes. We will point out instances and failures of conservative adharma. But we won't beat up on, condescend to, or fear those. We'll just try to help.

After all, we really are good guys, you know.

Unions

Unions – heroes or villains? Recently, Donkey Dharma was confronted with this question.

On May 17th 2010, we worked at the polls for the primary. As you might imagine for an off-year, local-stuff-only election, turnout was thin. Almost the only folks present were poll workers – us Democrats, and our Republican colleagues.

We got into a discussion about unions with one of the latter; the conversation centered on public employee unions. The exchange came to a screeching halt when the gentleman in question responded to our statement that unions aren't selfish but rather simply looking out for their members' interests, by declaring that the two are one and the same.

How do we contest this? Let us count the ways.

Semantically, this opinion holds not even a drop of water. According to the Merriam-Webster online thesaurus, synonyms for *selfish* include: egoistic, egomaniacal, egotistic, narcissistic, self-absorbed, … self-obsessed, self-oriented, and our personal favorite, _solipsistic_. Protecting the interests of workers cannot be considered any of these. One could make the case that these terms better fit the behavior of Governor Walker of Wisconsin, and that the conduct of public-employee unions in that context might better be described by such synonyms for _reasonable_ as commonsense, firm, informed, justified, sensible, sober, solid, valid, and well-founded.

Politically, this position reflects the not-completely-uncaring but certainly insensitive attitude of many on the right. In a nutshell, their argument is: _Well, we're sorry if you weren't able to realize, as fully as you'd hoped, the American dream. But time waits for nobody. Those who made it big made it big. Those who didn't will just have to bear the weight of their own shortcomings or bad luck._ So much for compassionate conservatism.

Class Warfare

At Donkey Dharma, we're proud of being from Western Pennsylvania. (Google **North Braddock** when you have a chance.) We think often and fondly of our working-class upbringing; of the ethnic diversity and harmonious interaction between disparate groups that, until adulthood took us to another part of Pennsylvania, we considered the way of the world at large; and of the fact that, contrary to the pronouncements of many a cable news chatterer, working-class, proud-of-their-backgrounds Americans are also quite often progressives. (Google **Charles Owen Rice**.)

We're also saddened. Rightisimos like to accuse progressives of engaging in "Class warfare!" almost as much as they try to paint us as "Socialist!" But it is the working- and middle-class families of this country that have paid the price, actual and metaphorical, of conservatives' tax cuts for the wealthy, and of their readiness to gut regulatory agencies of all stripes.

Lest you think such policies a thing of the past, note this quote from John Boehner, Minority Leader in, and Speaker Wannabe of, the House of Representatives. Should the GOP regain control of the House (and hand the Speaker's gavel to – shudddder – Mr. Perpetual-Tan), he stated that "We are going to do everything we can to make sure that this law [health care reform] and this program never really takes effect." Seniors, get ready to pay back that $250.00 …

During the same interview, Mr. Boehner expressed strong support for the ongoing military effort in Afghanistan. The Representative seeks to ensure that there's enough money to keep our country in a state of endless war by "reforming" the country's "entitlement system": increasing the Social Security retirement age to 70 for people who have at least 20 years until retirement; tying cost-of-living increases to the consumer price index rather than wage inflation; and limiting payments to "those who need them".

Mr. Boehner gave no hint as to how or by whom this determination of financial need would be made.

Hating President Obama

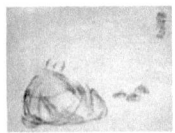

Why do wingnuts so loathe Barack Obama?

We think the answer's simple. He's black, intelligent, and progressive. And most anathematic to the crazed right, he's unafraid.

Imagine being so enshrouded in fear that anything that suggests hope must be attacked. Consider how it must feel to hate, in the belief that doing so denotes strength. When the President and the Democrats succeeded in passing health care reform and Wall Street reform and an extension of unemployment benefits, the right really saw red, and doubled down their efforts to alarm and divide.

Statements like Sharon Angle's "Second Amendment remedies" engendered this frightening event, as reported by the San Francisco Chronicle. Convicted felon Byron Williams loaded up his mother's Toyota Tundra with guns, strapped on his body armor and headed to San Francisco ... with one thing in mind: to kill workers at the American Civil

Liberties Union and an environmental foundation, prosecutors say. Williams, an anti-government zealot ... had hoped to "start a revolution" with ... bloodshed at the ACLU and the Tides Foundation ...

(See: http://www.sfgate.com/cgi-bin/article.cgi?f=/c/a/2010/07/21/MNMN1EHB37.DTL)

Mr. Williams envisioned starting a revolution. Andrew Breitbart may secretly have hoped to set off a race war with his utterly unconscionable edited-to-evoke-animosity video of Shirley Sherrod. Mr. Breitbart has been termed "almost sociopathic" by progressive bloggers. We concur. As evidence, we cite another Breitbart rant, in which he suggests that the farmer's wife who spoke out in defense of Ms. Sherrod is a "plant". (Heaven forfend that real people should affirm reconciliation ...)

(See: http://thinkprogress.org/2010/07/21/breitbart-farmers-wife-hoax/)

While the Administration was initially taken in by the Breitbart post, members eventually handled the situation with a grace and dignity Mr. Breitbart could not muster. Secretary of Agriculture Tom Vilsack said "I asked for Shirley's forgiveness, and she was gracious enough to extend it to me. ... This is a good woman. ... She has been put through hell. I could have done and should have done a better

Hating President Obama

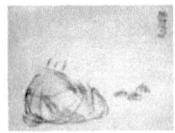

Why do wingnuts so loathe Barack Obama?

We think the answer's simple. He's black, intelligent, and progressive. And most anathematic to the crazed right, he's unafraid.

Imagine being so enshrouded in fear that anything that suggests hope must be attacked. Consider how it must feel to hate, in the belief that doing so denotes strength. When the President and the Democrats succeeded in passing health care reform and Wall Street reform and an extension of unemployment benefits, the right really saw red, and doubled down their efforts to alarm and divide.

Statements like Sharon Angle's "Second Amendment remedies" engendered this frightening event, as reported by the San Francisco Chronicle. Convicted felon Byron Williams loaded up his mother's Toyota Tundra with guns, strapped on his body armor and headed to San Francisco ... with one thing in mind: to kill workers at the American Civil

Liberties Union and an environmental foundation, prosecutors say. Williams, an anti-government zealot ... had hoped to "start a revolution" with ... bloodshed at the ACLU and the Tides Foundation ...

(See: http://www.sfgate.com/cgi-bin/article.cgi?f=/c/a/2010/07/21/MNMN1EHB37.DTL)

Mr. Williams envisioned starting a revolution. Andrew Breitbart may secretly have hoped to set off a race war with his utterly unconscionable edited-to-evoke-animosity video of Shirley Sherrod. Mr. Breitbart has been termed "almost sociopathic" by progressive bloggers. We concur. As evidence, we cite another Breitbart rant, in which he suggests that the farmer's wife who spoke out in defense of Ms. Sherrod is a "plant". (Heaven forfend that real people should affirm reconciliation ...)

(See: http://thinkprogress.org/2010/07/21/breitbart-farmers-wife-hoax/)

While the Administration was initially taken in by the Breitbart post, members eventually handled the situation with a grace and dignity Mr. Breitbart could not muster. Secretary of Agriculture Tom Vilsack said "I asked for Shirley's forgiveness, and she was gracious enough to extend it to me. ... This is a good woman. ... She has been put through hell. I could have done and should have done a better job." Press Secretary Robert Gibbs said "Members of this administration … have … made determinations and judgments without a full set of facts. … I think, without a doubt, Ms. Sherrod is owed an apology."

Too often at Donkey Dharma we feel we leave you with a hope deficit. Recognizing and acknowledging problems is of course important. But applauding those who grow from "teachable moments" – in this case Ms. Sherrod herself, as well as Mr. Vilsack and Mr. Gibbs – is important too.

19th Century Social Policies

Fear and hatred are becoming palpable in this country. One of us at Donkey Dharma noted recently "There's not much distance between that and what the Repugs preach."

"That" was the gut-wrenching film "The Stonng of Soraya M.". The final fifteen or so minutes of this movie depict in gory but necessary detail the execution by stoning of a woman in Iran. Her crime? None, other than refusing her abusive husband a divorce, and thereby preventing him from marrying a 14-year-old who'd caught his eye. The charges against her? Completely fabricated accusations of adultery.

That can never happen here, you're thinking. We hope you're right. But recent statements by citizens of Wingnuttia give us pause. Take, for example, the idea broached by one Republican who talked about rounding up the poor and sending them to prisons, where they could be "taught" useful "skills" and learn about more basic things like "personal hygiene". If that's not freakazoid enough for you, how about the 42 amendments to the Constitution proposed by conservatives since Barack Obama took office? Among these amendments are changing the constitution to suit their 19th-century social policies. Then of course we have the now-classic statements of folks like Sharon Angle regarding the need to "personalize" Social Security, and elaborating on the ways in which unemployment insurance makes those who are out of work "spoiled".

Do these people have no compassion at all? Are they so out of touch with the world around them that they can spout such drivel without rancor?

After the 2010 Midterms

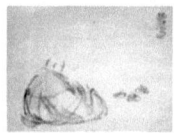

OMG, what was the BFD? What caused the rout Democrats suffered in the midterm elections on November 2nd? Sometimes explanations are merely facile, not informative. But that caveat doesn't apply to the events of 11/02.

Demographically, those midterms were dominated by older white people who are apparently very afraid or very gullible, or both. According to Ed Rendell, the soon-to-be-ex-governor of Pennsylvania, "Democrats acted like wussies. They didn't sell their legislative accomplishments." In other words, the white senior citizens who handed John Boehner the Speaker's gavel hadn't been fed sound bites that convinced them the Obama administration and the Democratic Party had done anything for them. Similarly, the "youth" vote never materialized. Apparently, more than a third of voters 30 or under still basked in the warmth of "Yes we can", and so neglected to put a few more logs on the fire of 2010. "Yes we can" became "We already did, and what a rush it was, and isn't my new SmartPhone cool?"

Voting is like fixing the bed, or doing the dishes, or brushing your teeth – very mundane, and very important. Buddhism teaches us to honor every aspect of life, even the mundane – especially, in some cases, the mundane. The midterm elections of 2010 were such a case. Assume the following:

- An estimated total number of votes cast in each of the recent PA Senatorial, PA7th House, and PA 10th House races of 2, 200,000
- An increase of 5% (from the 11% actual portion they formed of total voter turnout in 2010, but still less than the 18% they made up in 2008) of voters 30 and under
- An increase of 5% (from the actual percentage of 47% of white senior citizens who voted for Democrats in 2010, as opposed to the 57% who did so in 2008)

Under these assumptions, we'd be celebrating Senator Sestak and Representatives Lentz and Murphy, instead of looking for a beer to cry into. How to accomplish that?

Democrats must practice regular and ongoing outreach to both seniors and youngsters. Democrats must trumpet messages like "We're the party of the middle class; we believe we have to build our way out of our current fiscal troubles, not give tax breaks to people like

Warren Buffett." (By the way, Buffett himself says he doesn't need the tax breaks, and that those breaks won't trickle down and never have.)

To paraphrase the sage Pogo, "Progressives, we have met the enemy, and he is us."

became "We already did, and what a rush it was, and isn't my new SmartPhone cool?"

Voting is like fixing the bed, or doing the dishes, or brushing your teeth – very mundane, and very important. Buddhism teaches us to honor every aspect of life, even the mundane – especially, in some cases, the mundane. The midterm elections of 2010 were such a case. Assume the following:

- An estimated total number of votes cast in each of the recent PA Senatorial, PA7th House, and PA 10th House races of 2, 200,000
- An increase of 5% (from the 11% actual portion they formed of total voter turnout in 2010, but still less than the 18% they made up in 2008) of voters 30 and under
- An increase of 5% (from the actual percentage of 47% of white senior citizens who voted for Democrats in 2010, as opposed to the 57% who did so in 2008)

Under these assumptions, we'd be celebrating Senator Sestak and Representatives Lentz and Murphy, instead of looking for a beer to cry into. How to accomplish that?

Democrats must practice regular and ongoing outreach to both seniors and youngsters. Democrats must trumpet messages like "We're the party of the middle class; we believe we have to build our way out of our current fiscal troubles, not give tax breaks to people like

Warren Buffett." (By the way, Buffett himself says he doesn't need the tax breaks, and that those breaks won't trickle down and never have.)

To paraphrase the sage Pogo, "Progressives, we have met the enemy, and he is us."

We Got Him

Watching Rachel Maddow on the evening of Monday, May 2nd, we saw video of a crowd that had gathered at Ground Zero in New York City to celebrate the killing of Osama Bin Laden. One person in the crowd proudly waved a hand-lettered-in-magic-marker sign that read **We got him. Celebrate America**.

Don't get us wrong. At Donkey Dharma as everywhere, Osama Bin Laden was and is viewed as an international criminal. His death will (hopefully) make the United States and the world safer. But we were disturbed by the crowds' (at Ground Zero, in Times Square, at the White House, and doubtless at many other locations) chanting USA! USA! as if they were spectators at a sporting event. And we were really disturbed by that sign.

There are so many beautiful, enjoyable, noble things about this country that deserve to be celebrated, like:

- a child's hearing five languages other than English on the single block on which she spent the first thirteen years of her life

- attending a naturalization ceremony

- baseball

- blues and R & B

- the Constitution

- the inauguration of President Obama

At Donkey Dharma, we'd like to see crowds gather spontaneously to celebrate one of those.

Another Battle in Class Warfare

The New York Times recently reported that businesses' spending on machinery and technology has increased 26 percent, while spending on employees has inched up just 2 percent. Costs are, of course, a big factor: Labor costs have increased by nearly 7 percent during the nascent economic recovery we're supposedly experiencing, while equipment costs have declined. The Times reported further that the hoped-for rebound in workers' income share after the early 2000s recession never materialized, and that as a result this figure is now at its lowest level since the Bureau of Labor Statistics began tracking it in 1947.

But rather than an exception, workers' exclusion from the benefits of the recovery may constitute an alarming trend. A smaller and smaller share of the nation's income has gone to workers in recent years:

Compare these increasingly diminishing returns for workers to the steadily increasing ones for those who "labor" in the financial industry.

Class warfare indeed …

American Bigotry Travels to Norway

Buddhists hold that everything is connected to everything else. This premise is even the basis for a joke: "What did the Buddhist monk say to the hot dog vendor"? "Make me one with everything."

What isn't a joke is that hateful talk begets violent actions. Specifically, the anti-Islamic rhetoric of the wingnut American right, far from falling only on the ears of their brethren in bigotry, contributed to the recent horrific events in Norway.

The New York Times reports: "The man accused of the killing spree in Norway was deeply influenced by a small group of American bloggers and writers who have warned for years about the threat from Islam, lacing his 1,500-page manifesto with quotations from them, as well as copying multiple passages from the tract of the Unabomber. In the document he posted online, Anders Behring Breivik, who is accused of bombing government buildings and killing scores of young people at a Labor Party camp, showed that he had closely followed the acrimonious American debate over Islam. " Read the entire Times piece at:

http://www.nytimes.com/2011/07/25/us/25debat e.html?_r=1

We must remain alert to the possibility, always present, of demagoguery and hatemongering inciting violence. Universally, people engaging in such behavior shirk all responsibility for events like those in Oslo. We must not let them off the hook. Every day, in whatever circumstances we find ourselves, we must respond to words or actions grounded in fear and hate with firmness and an affirmation of what is right.

The Poor

Some scholars believe that, during the 18 years not reported on in any of the Books of the New Testament, Jesus travelled to the East, and interacted with Hindu and Buddhist teachers. Perhaps it was during that period that he developed the idea that there will always be those who live in poverty.

But at Donkey Dharma, we cannot believe that he meant by that to justify in any way practices that engender and deepen poverty. Practices like those of de-regulated banks and run-amok hedge funds that have managed to gut the real incomes of all but the wealthiest Americans.

Since 1947, the working population of the United States has lost rather than gained income.

Jesus said "The poor you will always have with you …" (Matthew 26:11; Mark 14:7). He did not say "The poor will always exist and will become more and more destitute".

Economic Mobility, but in What Direction?

Want to be rich? In the United States, to fulfill that dream, you'd better be born rich.

The image below compares upward economic mobility in the United States to that in several other Western, industrialized countries.

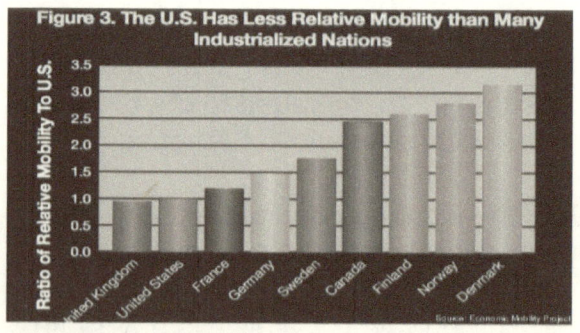

Apparently, many Republicans, including budget wonk Paul Ryan, haven't seen this chart. All GOPers tout the wonders of a trickle-down economy. Ryan recently gave a speech at the Heritage Foundation (opus of Richard Mellon Scaife) in which Ryan claimed that many governments constitute "top-heavy welfare states [which] have replaced … traditional aristocracies, and masses of … long-term unemployed are locked into the new lower class. The United States [has broken] out of this bleak history."

Uhm – Mr. Ryan – there's this chart …

The full report, of which the chart is only one small piece, can be found at:

http://www.scribd.com/doc/70425671/Economic-Mobility

Social Justice

We hold these truths to be self-evident, that all men are created equal, that they are endowed by their creator with certain inalienable rights; that among these are life, liberty, and the pursuit of happiness ... that it is to ensure these rights that governments are constituted among men, deriving their just power from the consent of the governed ...

At Donkey Dharma, we find that an excellent description or definition of social justice. Any society that lives up to that standard must, one would think, be just. Sadly, as the Bertelsmann Social Index reported on HuffPost World, and as Repugs have taken care to ensure, that thought would be without a basis in fact.

Jefferson, Franklin, and Adams would be distressed to learn that Bertelsmann ranks the United States 27th out of 31 nations in such facets of social justice as health care and income equity.

Not Right, but Rather Cruel, Speech

The third step on the Buddha's eight-fold path to enlightenment is called right speech. Buddhists understand right speech as meaning abstaining from lies, abstaining from slander, refraining from using malicious language, avoiding harsh words that offend or hurt others, and foregoing chatter that lacks purpose or depth. In a nutshell, this means telling the truth, and speaking with kindness.

Pennsylvania Governor Tom Corbett should reflect on the concept of right speech. Had he done so, he might not have made the incredibly insensitive comment he uttered a few weeks ago, regarding Pennsylvania's requiring medically unnecessary sonograms for women seeking abortions: "Just close your eyes." Given the definition of right speech, Corbett struck out four out of five times.

Nor can we assume that the presumptive Republican Presidential nominee, Mitt Romney, would be any better a practitioner of right speech. On April 17th, Gov. Corbett endorsed Mr. Romney, as follows.

> *Now that the long primary season has ended, it is time for Republicans to come together and unite around the one candidate who can defeat Barack Obama and institute a bold conservative vision that we need in Washington. That is why I am heartily endorsing Mitt Romney. Our country needs a president who will reverse President Obama's failed policies and ensure an opportunity for all Americans to prosper. Mitt Romney will restore fiscal sanity to Washington by cutting spending, lowering taxes, and reforming entitlements.*

In our mind. "bold conservative vision" = "just close your eyes". The insensitivity of Gov. Corbett's remarks and attitudes bodes poorly for the approach of his new BFF Mitt Romney. That's why we think "cutting spending" = "shafting those in need", that "lowering taxes" will apply only to the rich, and that "reforming entitlements" = "Goodbye Medicare and Medicaid". So much for right speech …

Diversity

One of Donkey Dharma's dads had a metaphor for a fruitless effort – *like a blind chicken looking for corn*. That pretty well sums up the search for right speech in today's polarized American politics.

Republican Congresspeople and talking heads obstinately fan the flames of fear by questioning President Obama's citizenship and therefore his legitimacy. We have compassion for these folks. They must feel like merde inside, to construct more and more elaborate conspiracy theories, to cling so desperately to the hope that their world view, dominated by white literalist Christian people and beliefs, is not being replaced by something more inclusive, by something which appreciates rather than fears diversity.

Growing up in a steel town in western Pennsylvania did not teach such views or fears.

On the one block on which one of us spent the first 13 years of life, five languages other than English (German, Italian, Slovak, Hungarian, and Polish) were heard regularly. Every ethnic group had its place of worship – German, Polish, Irish, Italian, Ruthenian, Croatian, Serbian, Hungarian, African-American, and Jewish. Almost everyone was working class, with U S Steel, the Pennsylvania Railroad, and Westinghouse dominating. The result? Diversity and cultural affiliation lived comfortably side by side.

That's a vision of America that scares the living daylights out of some. All we can do is counter their fear with facts, firmly but without rancor. Imagine how much more vital our political life would be if even a few of the fearful moved past their anxiety to acceptance.

Elizabeth Warren

We at Donkey Dharma fancy ourselves wordsmiths. But we couldn't have said it better ourselves.

It being Elizabeth Warren's recent right speech regarding the social contract that supports American society. Here is that statement, nearly in its entirety.

> *I hear all this, you know, 'Well, this is class warfare, this is whatever … No. There is nobody in this country who got rich on his own. Nobody.*
>
> *You built a factory out there? Good for you. But I want to be clear: you moved your goods to market on the roads the rest of us paid for; you hired workers the rest of us paid to educate; you were safe in your factory because of police*

forces and fire forces that the rest of us paid for. You didn't have to worry that marauding bands would come and seize everything at your factory, and hire someone to protect against this, because of the work the rest of us did.

Now look, you built a factory and it turned into something terrific, or a great idea? God bless. Keep a big chunk of it. But part of the underlying social contract is you take a hunk of that and pay forward for the next kid who comes along.

Bravo, and about time.

Right Speech and the Second Amendment

Right speech involves, not only refraining from outright lies or slanders, but also avoiding language that misleads, or clouds understanding.

Take the Right's misinterpretation of the Second Amendment. Our conservative brethren insist that this part of the Bill of Rights offers carte blanche for guns. No rules, no constraints – go out and buy the biggest, most lethal, most bad-ass firearm you can find. The Founding Fathers wanted every American to be able to own an Uzi.

And so today there are 90 guns for every 100 Americans.

You might wonder "In what way do conservatives misinterpret the Second Amendment?" Let's start with the Amendment itself.

A well-regulated militia, being necessary to the security of a free State, the right of the people to keep and bear arms, shall not be infringed.

Note the punctuation and the semantics created thereby. Note also the mention of "a well-regulated militia". The latter is significant. At the time of the writing of the Constitution, and for some years thereafter, the United States had no standing army. It had no choice but to rely upon its militias. That's where the punctuation and resulting semantics kick in. It would be completely correct linguistically to paraphrase the Second Amendment as saying "Since we need a militia to protect ourselves, we won't prevent citizens from keeping and bearing firearms."

That logic no longer applies. The United States has the largest, most technologically advanced, and best-trained military in the world. It has, too, the 21st century equivalents of a well-regulated militia, in the National Guard and Reserves. It has police forces at the Federal, state, and local levels. All of these bodies are more-than-well armed.

It's time either to reinterpret, or to supersede, the Second Amendment. Too many guns by far, and too many Americans celebrating that fact.

We're All Sikhs

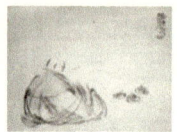

In the 1930s, they burned crosses in Munhall, on the hills behind and above the home of one of Donkey Dharma's grandmothers. In that same era, one of our grandfathers sat on his front porch in Holmes with a shotgun across his lap, knowing the Klan was on its way.

In Munhall in the Pittsburgh area, Slavs were hated. In Holmes in southeastern Delaware County, the Irish were the object of contempt.

Fast forward to today. In Wisconsin, Sikhs, because their skin is slightly darker, because some of their men wear turbans, became the prey of someone deeply involved in the skinhead far right.

Our well-worn copy of the Constitution sits on the kitchen table in front of us as we type this, open to the First Amendment. Freedom of speech and of the Press should remain sacrosanct. But we can't help but feel that the Michele Malkins and Matt Drudges and Glenn Becks and Rush Limbaughs of our society bear part of the responsibility for what happened in Oak Creek. Broadcasting (literally and figuratively) hate begets actions like those taken at the Sikh temple. Malkin, Drudge, Beck, Limbaugh, et al should be held responsible, ethically, and even, if possible, legally.

The Politics of Jesus

The concept of sangha, or community, is central
to Buddhism. Sangha can mean anything from
a group of like-minded spiritual practitioners to
the collection of one's neighbors and fellow
citizens.

America today fails at being a sangha in either
sense. As a national community, we're
polarized financially, politically, and socially.
Our neighbors on the right tout "Christian
values", wave the banner of morality, and use
both to fan the flames of fear and distrust, while
simultaneously claiming to be the only ones
acting out of concern for the public.

Progressives have any number of parries and
ripostes to this faux righteousness. In his book
"The Politics of Jesus", Rev. Obrey Hendricks
provides a particularly cogent one.

Rev. Hendricks discusses the prophets of the
Old Testament. He notes that they and their

work arose at a time when Israel as a nation and a society had become highly stratified – the very rich few and the impoverished everybody-else – into an analog of our 1% versus 99%. It was in this context that authors of the Old Testament acted as prophets.

That role didn't require clairvoyance, foresight, or even good hunches. Rather, as Rev. Hendricks explains, the Hebrew word nadi was most frequently translated to the Greek prophetus, from which in turn we get the word we know.

But that word's Greek and Hebrew antecedents mean, not a psychic, but literally a spokesperson. Old Testament prophets like Amos and Ezekiel saw themselves simply as speaking out for the social justice their Creator required. They viewed their work as reminding the sangha that was the Kingdom of Israel that a 1% - 99% division of wealth and resultant opportunity just didn't cut it.

To consider ourselves, the sangha of progressives, as good guys, and our misguided conservative neighbors as bad guys, would be the height of moralistic pride. Nonetheless, we can pat ourselves on the back – vigorously. As spokespeople for the social justice the Creator demands, conservatives have nothing on us.

Laughable … at First

Buddhists, even more than many faith traditions, retain and value a sense of humor. So we think that Thich Naht Hahn, Pema Chodron, and others would smile, as we at Donkey Dharma did, at the latest wingnut conspiracy theory.

ThinkProgress.org reported that Tennessee state Rep. Kelly Keisling (R) is spreading to his constituents the theory that President Obama will fake his own assassination to avoid an election against Mitt Romney.

In an email sent from a government email address in his office, Keisling forwarded a warning that the President and the Department of Homeland Security are working together to raise the specter of white supremacist groups run amok, in order to justify implementing martial law, and heading off the November 6th election by pretending the President has been killed.

Indeed laughable. At first.

But sobering when one realizes how many of our brethren on the far right eat this stuff up. And more sobering still when one considers that some sad, damaged individual may hear this theory, believe it, and decide to act upon it.

Job-Creating Fund Raiser

Buddhism frowns upon what it calls dualistic thinking – what we would more likely refer to as black/white or right/wrong thought. Buddhists instead point out that nothing exists without being affected by the circumstances under which it arose or in which it finds itself.

Someone should mention that to the leader of the House Republican Job Creators Caucus, Rep. Reid Ribble (R-WI). Mr. Ribble recently distributed a press release that said in part "we've created a caucus for just about everything under the sun except creating a job. I hope this group of business-owners-turned-legislators can help fill that void." Then, the weekend of October 22nd, Ribble tweeted his constituents, promising a free jobs fair in Appleton, WI.

Trouble is, his office had also scheduled a $1,000/host ($100/guest) fundraiser, billed as a *Roundtable Discussion and Sporting Clays*

Tournament. Asked by a Fox affiliate about the Democratic complaint that Ribble had abandoned his own jobs creation event to tend to his campaign coffers, Ribble said it was probably best that he hadn't attended the jobs fair, since his having done so would have served as a distraction from folks needing jobs..

Not only dualistic but dishonest, insensitive, and self-centered. What a combination.

Lilly Ledbetter

In Buddhist fable and fact, there are many women who've done more than keep the hearth-fires burning. For instance, the school of kung fu practiced by Bruce Lee, called Wing Chun kung fu, was devised by a Buddhist nun. Today, Pema Chodron, a native New Yorker and graduate of UC Berkeley, is a prolific and highly-regarded author. (See: <u>Practicing Peace in Times of War</u>, Shambala Publications, 2007.) We think both Chodron and her predecessor the nun would understand and appreciate Lily Ledbetter.

Recent Repuglican efforts to return women to their not-so-distant-in-time roles as second-class citizens, to deny them not only rights but the dignity of self-actualization, haven't helped our benighted brethren on the right. No one better understands the reason for that than Ledbetter herself. Allow us to quote from her speech at the Democratic National Convention of 2012.

Women still earn just 77 cents for every dollar men make. Those pennies add up to real money. It's real money for the little things like being able to take your kids to the movies and for the big things like sending them to college. It's paying your rent this month and paying the mortgage in the future. It's having savings for the bill you didn't expect and savings for the dignified retirement you've earned.

Maybe 23 cents doesn't sound like a lot to someone with a Swiss bank account, Cayman Island Investments and an IRA worth tens of millions of dollars. But Governor Romney, when we lose 23 cents every hour, every day, every paycheck, every job, over our entire lives, what we lose can't just be measured in dollars.

Three years ago, the house passed the paycheck Fairness Act to level the playing field for America's women. Senate Republicans blocked it. Mitt Romney won't even say if he supports it. President Obama does. In the end, I didn't get a dime of the money I was shortchanged.

But this fight became bigger than Lilly Ledbetter. Today, it's about my daughter. It's about my granddaughter. It's about women and men. It's about families. It's about equality and justice.

This cause, which bears my name, is bigger than me. It's as big as all of you. This fight, which began as my own, is now our fight—a fight for the fundamental American values that make our country great.

We'd call that game, set, and match …

Still More Class Warfare

We've looked at the Buddhist concept of right speech before. In a nutshell, the paradigm seeks to induce us to tell the truth, but to do so without rancor.

By definition, then, right speech doesn't rule out frankness, or speaking truth to power. Consider this excerpt from a recent post at The Maddow Blog (http://www.maddowblog.msnbc.msn.com).

> *Welcome to class warfare, Republican style.*
>
> *In case anyone's forgotten, … millions of Americans may be exempt from income taxes, but they still pay sales taxes, state taxes, local taxes, Social Security taxes, Medicare/Medicaid taxes, and in many instances, property taxes. It's not as if these folks are getting away with something – the existing tax structure leaves them out of*

the income tax system because they don't make enough money to qualify. Indeed, many are retirees who can't earn an income because they're no longer in the workforce.

But for many Republicans, including the party's presidential candidate, it's "a real problem" that these folks aren't also paying federal income taxes – and the only way to correct this problem is by increasing the tax burdens of those least able to afford it.

As Americans and as aspiring bodhisattvas (look it up) we should be better than that …

The Second Amendment

Buddhists believe that undue attachment to ideas, even Buddhist ideas, can be as crippling as any other addiction. Keep that in mind in the context of the Constitution (a well-worn copy of which sits on the kitchen table here at Donkey Dharma HQ). Today's so-far-to-the-right-they-might-as-well-be-in-the-middle-of-the-Atlantic Republican Party regularly reveres that document. Our conservative brethren seem particularly fond of the Bill of Rights, and within that especially enamored of the Second Amendment.

The Second Amendment reads "A well-regulated militia, being necessary to the security of a free State, the right of the people to keep and bear arms shall not be infringed." Note that at the time of the writing of the Constitution, the Founders very strongly opposed maintaining a standing army; ergo the reasoning behind the Second Amendment. (Read some of Jefferson's thoughts on this topic, particularly those that equate organized military forces with tyranny.)

Notice also the Second Amendment doesn't mention AK47s or 30-round clips for a semi-automatic handgun. Just the need to defend the country, and the resultant and corollary need for citizens to own guns.

We'd like to suggest a different approach. Rather than clinging like white to rice to an originalist cum waaay-out-in-right-field view of the Constitution, why don't we simply adopt a second, and more relevant to our times, Bill of Rights?

Uhmm … actually, Franklin Roosevelt beat us to it. In his Second Bill of Rights, presented as part of his State of the Union speech of 1944, Roosevelt opined that citizens have a basic right to employment that pays a living wage, freedom from unfair competition and monopolies, decent housing, basic medical care, adequate education, and Social Security.

Profanity

Chris Hayes of MSNBC said, in a statement about the right of citizens to participate in their democracy, that it is "profane" to interfere with that effort.

Yet 16 states, all Republcan-controlled, instituted harsh voter-suppression laws. Here in Pennsylvania, home of Donkey Dharma, the law in question was stayed, and hopefully will not intimidate voters in 2012. But it certainly might confuse many, and thereby dissuade some from voting.

Hayes was right. It is indeed profane to try to interfere with what Representative John Lewis, a hero of the Civil Rights movement, called "the most powerful non-violent tool we have."

Right Speech by Representative Lewis. Definitely not Right Speech or Right Action on the part of those attempting to suppress votes or intimidate voters.

Etch-a-Sketching the Truth

Mitt Romney's Etch-a-Sketch campaign has been a resounding example of failing to adhere to Right Speech. Mr. Romney's practice of changing positions on every issue has earned him monikers such as "Jello Man" – not solid and substantial, but rather wiggly and soft.

The former Governor of Massachusetts went further in the last week of the Presidential campaign. He simply lied. He proclaimed that jobs producing Jeeps in Toledo Ohio were being outsourced to China. Chrysler responded with heated denials, but Mr. Romney persisted in his prevarications.

His utter inability and unwillingness to speak the truth, his insistence on saying whatever he thinks his audience du jour wants to hear, completely crushes the principle of Right Speech. It equally completely disqualifies him for the Presidency.

You Don't Have to be a Buddhist

Governor Chris Christie of New Jersey is known for speaking bluntly. His reputation might not seem to indicate adherence to Right Speech.

But after Hurricane Sandy hit New Jersey, Governor Christie was at his best. He chided Fox News talking heads for interjecting politics, and specifically the Romney campaign, into the discussion of the storm. Two days later, he praised President Obama and FEMA fulsomely, albeit with typical Christie straight-talk. "If I think he deserves praise, I'll praise him. If I think he deserves scorn, I'll give him scorn. But in this case he deservers praise."

It just goes to show you – you don't have to be a Buddhist to speak up for truth and fairness.

Not a Traditional America Anymore?

The day after the 2012 Presidential election, Bill O'Reilly opined "It's not a traditional America anymore."

Dog-whistle alert – boop, boop, boop! Dude, when was it ever a traditional AKA WASPM (white anglo saxon protestant male) America?

When Irish immigrants began arriving in the United States in the 1840s, attitudes like O'Reilly's made themselves known with signs in shop windows that read "No dogs or Irish allowed". Eastern European immigrants to Western Pennsylvania in the early 20th Century were met with another manifestation of fear- and hate-based attitudes. The Ku Klux Klan burned crosses on the hills above the immigrants' homes. And then, of course, there was the interning of Japanese Americans during World War II ...

O'Reilly's statement is one side of a coin that has as its other face the lawn sign "Take Back America". Dudes, it was never yours in the first place. America belongs to everyone.